Are

MW01531855

Buttons Red?

Are All My Buttons Red?

THOUGHTS FROM A CAREGIVER

Brenda Wiseman

Brenda Wiseman

Outskirts Press, Inc.
Denver, Colorado

The opinions expressed in this manuscript are solely the opinions of the author and do not represent the opinions or thoughts of the publisher. The author has represented and warranted full ownership and/or legal right to publish all the materials in this book.

Are All My Buttons Red?
Thoughts From A Caregiver
All Rights Reserved.
Copyright © 2011 Brenda Wiseman
v3.0

Cover Photo © 2011 JupiterImages Corporation. All rights reserved - used with permission.

This book may not be reproduced, transmitted, or stored in whole or in part by any means, including graphic, electronic, or mechanical without the express written consent of the publisher except in the case of brief quotations embodied in critical articles and reviews.

Outskirts Press, Inc.
http://www.outskirtspress.com

ISBN: 978-1-4327-6224-7

Outskirts Press and the "OP" logo are trademarks belonging to Outskirts Press, Inc.

PRINTED IN THE UNITED STATES OF AMERICA

DEDICATION

This book is dedicated to my dear friends Susan, Sally, Judy, Sheila, Sylvia, Karen and Inez who supported me through the years of caregiving and writing. To my brother, Larry, who loves me no matter what. To Lifepath Hospice who helped make Mom's last days the best possible. And to my Muse who wouldn't let me quit.

INTRODUCTION

Two months before Mom died she told me, "We didn't want you to move here, but you kept saying you just knew you needed to. You were right."

Divorced with no children, my job coming to its preordained end, and celebrating my 50th birthday, I took a deep breath and planned my next adventure. I decided it was time to move to Florida to take care of my parents. This decision to care for my parents always seemed to be there, a tiny thought that took root many years ago, waiting for its time to become a reality. Even though I felt the move was too soon, it seemed the smart thing to do. Go to Florida for the job search, instead of staying in Ohio, finding a job there, and then doing it all over again when the time was right. Little did I know that it wasn't too soon at all.

It took me time to realize I was right where I was

needed. It took time to come out from behind my sturdy wall of denial. Actually, I stepped out many times, only to zip back behind that wall, pretending everything was just fine. But it wasn't.

Dad was having trouble balancing the checkbook. As a former auditor he wouldn't admit it and couldn't accept it. Mom couldn't see well enough to put out her 14 daily pills, or quite remember what time of day to take them. Dad was not taking all his pills, because he was trying to save money. Mom's two front false teeth fell out, but she wouldn't get them replaced. With so many small things piling up around them, they were stuck and overwhelmed.

There were some things I could remedy immediately, and they allowed me to go ahead and take care of those things. There were some things I could remedy immediately; however, they would not, could not give up the control to allow me to help. Those things I monitored, while crossing my fingers and hoping all would be well. There were some things we could work through together and did, giving all of us a great feeling of accomplishment. Then there were the things we had to learn to live with and accept. As the 7½ years passed—this was our template for living and loving. We followed this plan, making sure life was good. My parents kept their dignity, I kept my

sanity, and all of us kept our sense of humor!
Dad died at home from a massive heart attack 2½
years after I moved to Florida. When it happened,
Mom was home by herself. I was on my way to
work. Mom died at home 5 years later, exactly 1
year after I resigned and 4 months of Hospice care.

I could not have handled these years without the
support of my brother, Larry, my "old" friends from
Ohio, my "new" friends in Florida, my e-mail, and
Hospice.

These thoughts are based on my journals and
emails from the time I made the decision to move
to Florida until the aftermath of both my parents'
deaths. I was incredibly lucky to have had this time
with both my Mother and Father, to resolve some
issues and to reconnect. The title comes from a
question Mother asked me one day. She looked
down at her robe and wondered, "Are all my
buttons red? " She looked at me with confusion
and I answered her with a, "Yes they are. Aren't
they pretty?" This exchange tells the story of
our caregiving journey. Asking questions and
accepting the answers with trust and love.

Because of family, friends and Hospice, my
Mother could say, "How can I be happy? I know I
am dying, but I'm happy."

"I am wondering where I will get the energy for this—the move, but that is just the beginning—finding a job—making new friends—taking care of Mom and Dad. How am I going to do that?"

The decision has been made. The journey begins. You have started asking the "hows" and feeling it's all so overwhelming. Overwhelming and scary, but that's OK—really. If you didn't feel either of these you would be missing the feeling of rightness deep in your gut. Somehow it just all comes together and gives you the big picture. The puzzle pieces fit, the picture emerges, and as the picture takes shape the path will be revealed.

With just a slight adjustment "scared" becomes "sacred," and the responsibility doesn't feel quite so heavy.

"It's Dad's birthday—77 years old—I never, ever imagined he'd make it this long—especially after his first heart attack, at what, 50? And that I soon turn 50."

The role of caregiver smacks you in the face with your own mortality. Mortality then flaunts its power by taking you on a roller coaster ride backwards, into the past then shoots you forward, into the future, with one of those 50 foot drops just for fun. The problem with this amusement park ride is it keeps you from being in the amazing present.

Did you ever think about the definition of "present"? It means: the here and now, a gift, or being there—or all three.

"50 sounds as if you are old and then 90 sounds very old—everything in between is gravy!"

Isn't it wonderful to share the gravy times together? We might not always agree on what ingredients to use or when to stir the pot. And sometimes that gravy will burn while we "discuss" the options, but because we are making it together, one very important ingredient is always there—love.

Even lumpy gravy can be delicious.

"Sometimes I wonder if I'll have another lover—but it is hard to think about that when staying in the here and now—which is the only way to do this moving away."

There is so much a caregiver must give up to actually give the care. It is too hard a job to believe it's just another duty being added to an already long list. So using careful thought, decide what will be the part of your life which must fade away for now. This realistic approach will save an incredible amount of energy and anguish.

Moving away also means moving toward.

"What a day this has been! Made over $1,000 today on the moving sale—I'm happy about having the money and I'm happy about not having to move all that stuff."

So much can happen when you rid yourself of all the things you don't need anymore. Clothes, books, preconceptions, attitudes. First you release the ones that don't work anymore and then you make room for the ones that do. There are many new and surprising developments just waiting for you, when you make room in your life.

Don't you wish we could get paid for all our unwanted "stuff"? We do.

"It's so quiet around here—I'm down to the last few things to do and the condo is so empty—and the weather is so heavy—I feel as if the sky is going to smother us all—guess that's why it's called a low."

Some days will feel so heavy it's almost impossible to lift your arms. And some days will feel so smothering you wonder if you'll ever breathe freely again. Then you will see that shimmering light of thankfulness in your loved one's eyes, even if fleetingly, and you know deep, invigorating breaths are on their way back—for both of you.

It's when you don't acknowledge the lows, that you can't imagine the highs. Especially if you don't imagine together.

"Saying goodbye was so much harder than I thought it would be."

You may never know how much you mean to others, even when you know you mean something. And it doesn't matter if you don't quite feel like smiling one day or you balk at getting out of bed to face the world, because there are those other days when there is nothing more you want to do than jump out of bed and smile. Honest.

It feels good to be loved and to love.

"The weather is awful—we may not be able to leave Thursday as planned."

"Going with the flow" may sound trite, but to caregivers, it is a guiding principle of daily life. Without this attitude, life is chaotic and it feels as if you are being pulled in too many directions. As you try to make sure all the pills are taken on time and all the meals are tasty, you can lose your energy. The one thing you need the most.

"As planned" must become synonymous with "flexible."

"I still have 'stuff' to do and I am running out of steam—so I'm going to change this outlook—if I talk myself into being tired and worn out, that certainly won't help anything. So-o-o up and at 'em."

Remind yourself that your attitude can be the difference between throwing the covers off and jumping out of bed or pulling the covers up over your head. We can talk ourselves into and out of the strangest places and if we are really good, we can take others with us. It's not ignoring what is "real," but hearing all the possibilities.

Talking to yourself can be very enlightening—as long as you make sure you're listening.

"The weather has been awful/wonderful—awful for traveling, but wonderful for beauty. Two to three feet of snow on the ground—it's quite a sight—and I love the way it effects the sound of things—so very, very quiet, muffled—silent."

Beauty is. You may see it when your Mother describes the brilliant orbs of light in her room and tells you they are souls. Or as your Father compares his bride, your Mom, to a robin redbreast. You may feel it as you hold a soft, fragile hand and just sit quietly together. Life is awful/wonderful.

Sometimes we get what we need, even when we don't know it.

"Left for Florida."

There will be times when "IT" just has to be done. Little Its and Big Its get you through another day, happily, peacefully, grandly or barely. However you get through that day, you made it. You got "IT" done.

Some days the "doing" will be all important—not the thinking or the feeling, but the action.

"This is the first day of waking up without a friend here—so it doesn't quite feel like vacation anymore, but it hasn't really sunk in that this is where I live."

It can take some time for changes to become as comfortable as those old shoes we always hear about. And as we wait for the comfort, it can be scary, then exhilarating, then confusing, then inspiring. But always, the journey is a privilege. The journey is what makes those old shoes comfortable.

"Sinking in" is the process of going from the head to the heart.

"It's good I am here—Mom and Dad are both relieved."

You will see how relief touches your parent—a relaxation around the mouth, a lowering of the shoulders, a tightness that softens. It is the beginning of the shift—responsibility, decision making, and labor—from the parent to the child. This shift signifies many changes to your life and your parents' lives.

Life is a cycle, so let's just keep pedaling.

"When I get a job—things will be different—as is everything."

Sometimes the difference you seek is a return to what used to be. Sometimes the difference you seek is knowing exactly how the future will unfold. However, the task is to take what is different and mold it into a comfort zone which allows the past to live and the future to be faced.

Everything changes—lucky for us.

"I need to acknowledge I am scared and then go through it—don't become frozen/paralyzed by it—don't let the fear overcome me. I need to do this for all kinds of practical reasons, but also for my own growth."

Fear is not something you tip your hat to in greeting and then move along never to run into each other again. It comes around on your path in many disguises. The important lesson, after you have acknowledged fear's existence, is to just keep on walking. Don't stand there arguing with your fear. That means you are stuck, fear has won, and you never complete the journey.

It is impossible to grow, if fear has you frozen.

"I need to start my new checking account and take another load to Goodwill. I am amazed at what Mom has kept—13 pair of tweezers! (Of course, I had 17 watches—ha!)"

Organizing the physical space gets you thinking in an organized way, grounding you. Organizing helps you dismiss all that is getting in the way and hindering you in becoming your most efficient. Thinking it through, making a plan, arriving at decisions that are the best for everybody. At least it did for me.

You cannot control time, no matter how many watches you own.

"The constant TV noise is going to get to me. That's what the great outdoors is for—and here I go!"

Getting away from the noise can be deeply important. All the noise—TVs, radios, requests from others, sighs and muted moans. You have to learn how to make static become soothing white noise, and how to pick up only the most important signals. Turning down the volume on your own noise isn't always easy, but the volume button is right in front of you for easy access.

The whole word is still out there—just waiting for you to take a break and help it celebrate.

"Mom has gone back to sleep—I wonder if she's ready for another transfusion."

You will learn more medical terms, read more charts and fill more prescriptions than you ever thought possible. It's as if more knowledge will make everything "OK." And as much as new knowledge will help you, remember the old—how much you love your Mom and Dad—how much you want what's right for them. Decisions will be easier to make with the old knowledge as well as the new. Not easy, but easier is good, too.

"I-wonder-if" is one of fears more gentle disguises.

"Dad fell out of bed and has been grunting and groaning—yelping actually—he doesn't want to go to the doctor—he isn't short of breath, so...."

It's difficult to realize that the protecting can become the problem. When what we think is protection takes on a life of its own, growing into Godzilla, stomping on feelings, thoughts and dignity, it is no longer helpful. So no matter how much we think a certain path should be followed, sometimes a different direction must be taken.

Protecting/smothering: a fine line, but a big difference.

*"I just can't believe how much I am like Mom—
and then how much I'm not like Mom. It's kind of
spooky."*

There will be many times the boundary between
yourself and your parents will be as smudged
as an erased chalk line. You will be their past.
They will be your future. And the present will
be intertwined. It is a magical time to see how
you have grown to be like your parents and to
understand where you have chosen to grow in
different directions.

*There is so much of ourselves to see when we look
into another's eyes.*

"I wondered how long it would take Dad to come back here and talk. He just can't stand not knowing what I am doing—either can Mom, actually."

Coming to terms with being "the child" is critical and demanding. It is amazing how fast you can revert to "kid" status and neither you nor your parents even realize it. Remember, you are becoming the decision maker—it can turn your world upside down, at least for awhile.

Parents are on a need to know basis, and they always need to know—no matter how old you are.

"I have a job interview already."

Already? Another change? Even for somebody who relishes change, so much at once can be daunting. A step back, a deep breath, and knowing it is all OK, can stop your head from spinning and your heart from pounding. I know, easier said than done, but it can be done.

When "Already?" becomes "All ready!" life is suddenly bigger and better.

"I wish I had some time by myself, but that just isn't going to happen—even if I stay in my room, they find excuses for knocking on the door."

When you first add caregiver to your definition of who you are, the freedoms and acts you have taken for granted may be the things that are missed the most. Life becomes very different. It takes time for it all to shake down and settle. As long as you don't ignore this fact—it will be fine.

Sometimes the best thing you can say about the day is, "I'm glad that's over!"

"Went to a drumming circle last night—it was fun and I picked up some literature about other things to do."

Never forget that there is fun and joy to be had. It may come in trying something completely new or it may come in treasured traditions. And never forget that this fun and joy are nourishing, good feelings. They are not feelings to hide or be ashamed of having. They are bright spots for everybody—caregiver and loved one.

We really are involved in the circle of life, let us find the joy.

"I wonder if I'll ever meet another man. There is something special about that mall energy, not mall, male. Of course, there is something about mall energy, too!"

Remembering that you can't provide all your own energy, meet all your own needs, or hide all your fears is only half the solution to being a loving caregiver. The other half of the solution is remembering not to expect yourself to provide all your own energy, meet all your own needs, or hide all your fears—and that is the more difficult half to remember.

Don't expect to do this all on your own—it wouldn't be good for anybody.

"I definitely want to go to the meditation group this Sunday—unless, of course, I am celebrating winning the lottery, but I'd probably need it just as much—if not more—then."

We can all acknowledge—hopefully with both our head and our heart—the need for support during the dark times. However, realizing we also need support during the light times is not so easily recognized. Emotions—good or bad, up or down—are stressful, and the more people sharing the emotions the less stress on one individual—including you.

Even Atlas would have appreciated other shoulders to help him hold the weight of the world.

"Guess Mom's still doing things the way we've always done things and who can blame her— those are still the 'rules' as far as she's concerned and I don't think there is a chance new 'rules' can take effect."

Family dynamics can play such a number on, well, the family! As roles in the family shift and change, relationships are effected. The way things have always been done may just not work anymore. It's the understanding of this dynamic which keeps the family from exploding.

The most dynamic families have love, not power, as their centers.

"Mom to doctor's for shot today and then we'll go to lunch—the mother/daughter bonding is nice—I do like it!"

What a wonderful time to reconnect. The simplest tasks can teach us the most enjoyable lessons. Doing what has to be done in a joyful manner enables us to share thoughts, feelings and laughter, which enables us to more easily share wishes and tears when those are what we so desperately need to be share.

Savoring the moment truly is the spice of life.

"I have a feeling I might be offered this job and it feels so ungrateful to be turning down jobs—it's like, what if I'm not offered another one? How can I be so arrogant as to refuse more jobs?"

When your heart and gut speak to you, it is always a good idea to listen. Even though an answer to a problem makes sense, appears logical, seems to be for the best, if it doesn't feel "right," look it over again. It could be that the "wrong" answer seems completely "right." Making sure your brain and your heart agree can prove to be a valuable tool in caregiving.

When you put a different label on a problem, it can cease to be a problem.

*"He (Dad) is trying to keep me home. And that will
not happen—that I am positive. In fact, it helps me
leave the house to do other things. There is a dark
and light side to everything—remember that."*

Anger, usually a misuse of energy, can be turned
around into useful energy, if we take a nice deep
breath and hold it for a second. We can use this
anger to motivate ourselves. As much as we don't
want it to happen, we will get angry, and we need
to do something with that anger, or it will burrow
deep into our heats and leave a gaping hole.
Holes in our hearts leave us weakened, making
our life as a caregiver so much more difficult than
it needs to be.

How can we enjoy starlight without the dark sky?

"I feel in complete control when I am driving and a bit of that doesn't hurt at all. I do need to feel as if I have control over something during this unsettled time."

Using small tricks to get through the chaotic times is a smart thing to do. If these gimmicks are used as stepping stones to a calmer time and not as a way to deny the turmoil, they can smooth the jagged edges of a difficult period.

What we control is our reaction to an incident— not what we feel, but what we do.

"Just got back from lunch and shopping with Mom. It's a nice thing to do—even fun in its way. I'm glad to be here now."

It will be the little things that keep you going and make you smile. Watching Mom dip onion rings into horseradish sauce, gobble them down and then look up with a big grin on her face is one of my favorites. It is also these little things that will be missed so very much.

Memories are what give a life dimension.

"I sure miss real talking—I keep referring to 'real' this and 'real' that. It's true though—it's as if this is all just not quite real."

Your definition of the world will change through your time as a caregiver. Some changes will be broad and loud—some will be subtle. All will be transforming. Watch as "real" shifts from substantial and oh-so important to genuine and heart-felt.

Changes will come and then even the changes will change—and all of it is real.

*"I am not even energetic enough to make my
famous lists of what to do—let alone do them."*

There will be times when it all just has to wait.
Times when you have to sit down. Times when
you have to walk outside and let the sunlight
touch you. Times when you need some quiet and
stillness. And you must learn to take these times
so you will be able to be there for the times that it
really can't wait.

There are times that cannot be found on a clock.

"I am still writing about losing weight and finding a job, because what I have been doing is finding weight and losing jobs—now there is symmetry to that."

Food is not your friend—it is a necessity. It is your power source, not your support system. Your friends and family will be your comfort, not the second helping of mashed potatoes or that bowl of ice cream before bed. Weighty matters are the caregiving duties—not you.

The nourishment you need comes from inside you—not from inside the refrigerator.

"I am needing guidance on what to do about Dad—he is depressed. Is it the glucose imbalance or the start of Alzheimer's? He is confused, forgetful and mean."

No matter the amount of medical jargon you learn, or how many medications you know inside and out, you will still need a doctor's knowledge. You know the symptoms and together with the doctor you can find the right method to ease the pain, making their quality of life better.

Assuming you already know the cause of a problem hinders you from finding all the right answers.

"Just now I had to referee. I feel like their mother!"

Getting in the "middle of it" can be at the top
of your job description. Especially if it means
containing the hurt and pain that can be inflicted.
Be aware of all the pain—physical, certainly,
but don't forget mental, emotional and spiritual,
too. And remember that some hurts are actually
making things better, like setting a broken bone.

*Referees wear black and white; however, decisions
may be cloaked in gray.*

"This is about me doing for them, because it just feels right no matter how much I complain—it still feels like the right thing!"

Staying connected to your heart makes slogging through the garbage in your brain a cleaner journey. Doesn't mean there won't be some ranting and raving to be heard or dirt to be swept away. It just means there are no echoes of that complaining reverberating in the garbage dump. The "rightness" has left no room for the echoes of complaining.

If you can't hear your heart messages, nobody can. What a waste that would be.

"So I shall live in the 'here and now' with the idea of getting to the 'there and then'."

As much as you prepare for the future, your feelings will find you. Ones you hadn't expected. Staying with the thoughts and emotions that are helpful in the "here and now" allow these positive emotions to continue into the "there and then." Using this positive energy allows you to persist in your efforts. Cherishing the time you have now, so you can also cherish it later, nourishes both you and your loved one.

Taking the right path does not necessarily make it the easy path.

"It is rainy and dreary. Mom and Dad are both asleep. I need to figure out how to handle my aging parents. I need to give a little more attention to these responsibilities."

For as long as you will be a caregiver, no matter how many days, weeks, months or years, you will be walking a line. The line between doing for your loved one and doing for yourself. Only you can know where that line is. Only you know when this line must change directions. Only you know how to walk your line. But there will always be others there to follow your lead and support your choices. Believe it!

Just remember, a line is not always straight. You need a line to form a circle, a spiral or even a tetrahedron.

"It is so quiet—I can't hear a voice. Any minute now one of the old guys is going to come out that door and onto the front porch—or they are both sleeping."

For a person who wants quiet and solitude, it can take even longer for caregiving to become a comfortable fit. And the same can be said for a person who wants talking and sharing. As long as we remain aware that our needs and wants may be different from our loved ones, we can hold to our dignity and offer them theirs.

What you miss the most will show up just when you need it the most.

"I'm like Mom—can't move a muscle."

Before you know it, fatigue can sneak up behind you and knock your legs right out from under you. You needed to stay late at work. You needed to make those cookies for the bake sale. You needed to go back to the pharmacy because they ran out of your prescription. When what you really **needed** was to take a nap for an hour.

What you need the most will show up just when you need it the most, too. This one is trickier to recognize.

"I just read over a year ago—some things don't change. Then things really change. Dad is dead. It's been over a month now."

As time passed, I would hear Mom honor my Father's life with comments relating to the things he loved or what would have deeply effected him. "I'm glad he wasn't here to witness 9-11. I wish he could have helped celebrate Tampa's Superbowl win! He would have loved having another great-grandson." I realize I now do the same for my Mother, honoring both of their lives by reminiscing and acknowledging how they effected me, our family and their friends.

Honoring and accepting our parents is how to honor and accept ourselves. Who are we if not half of our mothers and half of our fathers?

"It feels as if I need to 'unsitck' some flotsam and jetsam before I can focus—like a dog circling before lying down."

This flotsam and jetsam are called feelings. And maneuvering through them all can be overwhelming. The most important thing to remember is, don't judge your feelings. They truly are neither good nor bad. **Feelings just are—** and letting them flow is the only way to make sure they do not stick, causing you problems later. There is no room for new feelings, thoughts or emotions, if old ones have hardened to the point where they cannot be removed.

Isn't it amazing what you already knew when you look back?

"I can be here to support her, but I can't be her whole life—and don't want to be."

It's when we think we have life under control that it jumps up and bites us. The significant issues will show up again and again and again. Keeping our boundaries and yet being a caring caregiver, seems to be an issue which comes around often. One reason for this returning conundrum is— boundaries change. They are not static, as much as we might wish they were.

Boundaries are not to confine, but to protect.

"I am truly worried about Mom's memory loss. And I am truly worried that she has/is becoming my entire life."

We need stress in our lives. It is what keeps everything from falling over. Depending on how we respond to stress, it can help us or stymie us. We can spin around so stressed out, that we just become dizzy. Or, our stress is an alarm alerting us to what needs to be done—what will silence the clanging and the banging of that alarm? It can be hard, hard, hard to refrain from spinning; however, with practice and perseverance we **can** stop the spinning and do what needs to be done.

Stress loves taking center stage, but that makes us ignore the other characters in the play.

"I really can't believe how fast time is flying. How can I live in the here and now, when it is the past before I blink?"

I learned, as long as I was savoring the time with my Mother, it didn't matter what I labeled it. Even in the middle of chaos, if I just reminded myself how precious my time with Mom was, things just didn't seem so crazy. Unfortunately, I didn't really learn this lesson with my heart until closer to the end, but learn it I did.

We only have so much time with each other. We are responsible for how wonderful that time is.

"Need to call for Mom's prescriptions and balance her checkbook. Sounds as if staying for 7 weeks with Larry will be OK."

Sometimes creativity is needed to achieve the balance required for taking care of others. And it is an incredible help when other family members are involved. When solutions are good for everybody, it is a red letter day! Just as that illusive, perfect pie crust Grandma used to so tenderly concoct. It might not always happen, but there is always the possibility.

Magic is even more fun when it surprises you in the middle of an ordinary day.

"When will Larry get here and when will they leave? How long will Mom stay in Virginia? How long will I stay in Florida?"

Questions. We have to ask them, for without them how would we find any answers? Of course, assuming we already know the answers or discounting one received is not very helpful. Answers may come in many disguises. Answers may change from one day to the next. You may be lucky and find more than one right answer to the same question. All that matters is you keep asking and you keep listening with your head and your heart.

It would be awful if we stopped asking questions. Wouldn't it?

"Larry has come and gone and taken Mother with him. It is so hard to believe I am actually alone in the house."

I remember the first time Mother went home with my brother. The first thing I did was turn off all the TVs. The second thing I did, was put much of what I called clutter into the cupboards. The first thing I did the day before Mother came home was put much of what she called necessary back on the counters. The first thing I did the day she arrived home was give her a big hug and a kiss. In between those days, I enjoyed my freedom and she enjoyed her son and his family.

It truly is a matter of perspective.

"I am so exhausted that everything seems as if it is a battle."

And some days it is.

A battle can only happen when there are two resisting forces.

"Part of me is just not here—maybe I feel I don't have the right to 'waste' time playing, because I have so many other things I need to be doing—cleaning, making doctor appointments, etc., etc."

Necessary and unnecessary suffering is found throughout life. We seem to hunt out the unnecessary suffering with uncanny accuracy and then use it to make ourselves feel even worse. We must learn to recognize the differences so we can ignore the unnecessary suffering. We owe it to ourselves as caregivers and to our loved ones who are the innocent bystanders in danger of being hurt.

A mantra of "I don't have the right to..." will make it the truth. Change that mantra!!

"I am feeling so out of control where Mom is concerned, her health, her mental capabilities, her depression. Feeling I am putting my life on hold. That really is something I do have control over—something I can control—my attitude."

Caregiving is the ultimate test for knowing there are just some things you can't control, and it is the ultimate opportunity to control what you truly can. You cannot control the progression of the disease, but you can control your reaction to the disease. You cannot control your feelings—and there are plenty of them. But you can control your attitude about those feelings. You can control what you do because of those feelings.

Making choices that are best for all—now that is control.

"It has been a year since Dad died—I feel sad Mom is not talking about it much and feel a bit guilty, too."

Time is so allusive. It can feel as if a major event happened just yesterday or as if it was so long ago it is difficult to remember. I think it has to do with memories, healing, guilt, questions, viewpoint, love. I just haven't discovered the formula yet. Everybody has to discover their own formula. We can share the mathematics, but each answer is unique.

You cannot hold back tears and breathe at the same time.

"Thinking about Dad's death makes me think about Mom's and how sad having her gone will be."

No amount of thinking has approached the reality. Not one thought included how the death of the second parent would magnify the loss of the first. Not just Dad or not just Mom, but the pair, the unit, is gone from the family circle. Who will tell the family stories in old photos?

It is never too late to find a new understanding.

"Mom is driving me to distraction—or I am letting her drive me. I am ready to take a nap—maybe I will, before going to work tonight."

One of the pit stops on the road to Distraction might really be just where you need to be. It's always a good thing to remember, some of the best times can be found when you are lost.

It's really important to know who is in the driver's seat. If you don't know you are driving you can't put on the brakes.

"Got two ambulance bills yesterday—one from the day Dad died and then a bill for my broken ankle."

Ah, those days of anger can and will show up at any time. And just when you thought you'd worked through it all. Whether your loved one's death is sudden, or a lengthy process, you may experience a feeling of "I-could-have-done-more." Also known as guilt. Just remember to forgive and love yourself, too.

Time is like a rubberband, sometimes stretching and sometimes snapping.

"It is Ma's birthday—81. I wonder how many more she will celebrate. I wonder if she wonders. I wonder how many more I will celebrate. I wonder if she wonders if I wonder."

Life is truly like an onion—layer upon layer upon layer—and peeling those layers can bring tears to your eyes. However, when the pieces of onion are added to the right mix, it tastes delicious. And just as the onion, life can be tasty raw, or sautéed, or chilled, but without peeling that first layer, it can't be used.

There's so much to taste and so many ways to taste it.

"Mundane things are going through my head, but I don't want to write those down—if I get rid of the mundane, then I'd have to face some real feelings."

Coping mechanisms are truly amazing. We learn what works to get us through the pain and then we learn when it is time to relinquish that method so we can face what is happening. This doesn't mean it is easy. This doesn't mean we do not fight it. But it does mean we are learning and growing and coping.

Don't let your coping mechanisms turn you into a mechanical toy.

"If I am going to wish for something, make it something that could happen now or in the future not waste a wish on the past—something that cannot possibly be changed."

When we find our energy running low, wishing for changes which cannot happen is a double whammy. It wastes our precious energy, and puts us in a place where we worry about what has been, instead of concentrating on what needs to be.

Wishes are great, as long as they don't stop us from living.

"I don't like confrontation, but it seems as if there is confrontation all around."

There are four definitions for "confront" in my dictionary and only one of them uses the word "antagonistically." Antagonistic is a hard word, an in your face word, a right-or-wrong word. When I decided to go with the fourth definition, "to set side by side to compare," how it softened my outlook. Even my physical stance changed from in your face to side by side. So much more can be accomplished softly.

Small changes can bring huge gains.

"I don't want Mom to suffer—for her or for me. Could I handle it?"

It is amazing what you can do when it is right there and must be handled. Looking back you may wonder how you did it. How did you hold your loved one's hand during the pain without totally collapsing? How did you smile while your heart was breaking? And in the end, it doesn't matter how, it only matters that you did.

The answer is, "Yes, I can handle it."

"My nomadic spirit is ready to go, but I won't be doing that."

Acknowledging our wants—specifically the ones we have put on hold—is being gentle with ourselves. To pretend these wants do not exist will lead to resentments, which when felt for too long can only lead to pain. We need to believe there will be another time for us to follow another path.

As time passes, some things which were so important to us can vaguely be recalled.

"My organizing, factual brain likes the computer. My creative, feeling, spontaneous brain likes the pen and paper. Printed words help me muddle through life. That's why I love books so much—the feel of the paper, and the letters and the spaces and the punctuation marks."

It is so easy to allow the "factual brain" to take control. If I just construct the perfect list, build a foolproof schedule, mark everything on the calendar, it will all be OK. And although all these tangibles are important, without compassion, life is sterile and removed. A caregiver who combines the factual with the spontaneous—the schedule with the compassion—is a caregiver who is giving the best care to their loved one and to themselves.

Feelings are the punctuation marks of life.

"Being true to myself—doing what feels right in the gut—not doing out of fear or 'shoulds'."

This path we travel with our loved one can be a scary path, but fear cannot be the motivator as we make decisions. When we make a decision out of fear, we are usually running away and running away wastes energy. We need to make choices which will help, or at least not hurt.

The "shoulds" will get you, if you don't watch out.

"Tomorrow—it makes me laugh as I write this. How many times have I said 'tomorrow'? Why not today?"

Really believing that we only have today is a lesson which must be learned over and over. No matter how many "todays" we have in a row, we have no guarantee the next "today" will arrive.

Living every "today" with love makes them all special.

"I want to quit saying, 'Who cares?' in such a way that means, 'I don't care.' What I really mean is, 'How is that important?' I am so depressed, trying not to pay attention when I need to pay attention. Time to eat some veggies!"

Humor is life confirming and sanity saving. It certainly is beneficial when admitting an unpleasant thought is the only thing you can do at that very moment. Humor can get you through the day as nothing else can, because there is nothing quite as intimate as a shared view of the world.

Nothing changes a person's looks as much as a smile.

"I am feeling a bit trapped, but what would I be doing now anyway? I hate feeling as if I am waiting for Ma to die, and what will be my purpose then?"

When the role of caregiver comes to an end and you sit down at the end of the day, don't be surprised if you are asking, "Who am I now?" Be gentle with yourself and don't feel guilty, for you have just lost much of what has defined you for many days. Give yourself time to think about this question.

Sometimes the best answers take time to be heard.

"Mom's pills—order—pickup—put out."

It's all a matter of perspective. How something so repetitive and boring, becomes something so repetitive and reassuring proves how changes in life can change a mind. Doing chores that were once mundane becomes a soothing ritual—familiar and needed. That chore can become a place of calm in the middle of turmoil and is no longer a chore.

Holding a "known" in your back pocket makes facing the "unknown" a bit less frightening.

"Mom was dusting last night, getting ready for the cleaning lady. Now how crazy is that?!"

Wanting to be useful is not crazy. Neither is wanting to be involved in life. Forgetting how important being useful and involved are just might be. There is so much more to dusting when it becomes so much harder to do.

Ridding yourself of your own cobwebs feels good and doing it as long as you are able, feels even better.

"Took Mom to the doctor's this morning and then out to breakfast. Pretty amazing!"

Days will come along that are so good and right you will just want to sing out loud. So you do—together! Being with your loved one, making time filled with laughter and easiness—there is nothing quite so beautiful as these shared moments. Remember to cherish them, for they truly are the light in the darkness.

Is there anything better than laughter, a light touch on the shoulder, a sharing of love?

"I hate telling Mom about things I've done, because she sucks out all the energy, dissects it, criticizes it, judges it and then goes into some long involved story of the olden days."

Days will also come along when you feel as if the whole day has been spent in a gigantic salad spinner. The faster it twirls, the more juvenile you feel and the tougher it is to keep those boundaries which you need to hold onto. All is a blur, so when it finally stops, which it will, and you recover from feeling dizzy, which you will, it is pure relief.

Being forced to take a long, deep breath may feel manipulative, but may be the very thing you need.

"It just doesn't seem possible how fast time flies. A minute ago it was Mom's 80th birthday party and now it is a month past her 81st birthday."

Mom told me she had never had a birthday party and sighed. So we planned a surprise 80th celebration. Of course, we had to tell her a few days before the big day so she could get her hair done and buy a new outfit. She was in her element that party day, simply glowing and greeting all her friends and family with hugs and kisses and huge smiles. Mom later told me it was the best day of her life. How lucky we were to be able to give her that day.

Listening to the smallest sound can lead you to the biggest discovery.

"What can I do to make now better—just do it and enjoy it! I'm waiting for somebody to cut the cast off from around my emotional self, when all my dreams are telling me to do it myself. "

If only all the world was black and white, knowing what you are responsible for would be so much easier. Of course, if you believe that we are all responsible for everything, then the world is in good shape and it can be any color you want.

Responsibilities are all in the eye of the beholder. If you see it, you are responsible for it.

"Mom seems to be slipping or I am just more nervous, maybe a bit of both. I am really going to need more help in handling my emotions and reactions and maybe getting out of denial. However, I still think she does some of these things knowingly and willingly."

Denial of what is or a continuation of family roles? My perception of events controlled my reactions to these events. Looking back, I see that the most frustrating times with Mom were at the half-way point from my arrival to her death. I wanted those nasty remarks to be deliberate, for if they were deliberate, this meanness wasn't indicative of a sliding and worsening of her health. It only meant she was cranky, her health was not getting worse, and we still had plenty of time.

Who's denying what? Short question. Complicated answer.

"Friday is the chorus concert—Mom and I have tickets. I wonder if she will really go?!"

Waiting must become an art. It is the space where the best moments can live. Waiting is the place you can catch a breath and a relaxing thought before the next wave hits. Without the periods of waiting, the "doing" would never end. The "doing" would grind you down. Waiting is a gift, not a cause for frustration.

Yes. No. Maybe. Going with the flow means accepting the path.

*"The word for today is 'distressed'—almost
'depressed,' but certainly 'stressed'."*

A. Distressed, "troubling to the mind or emotions."
B. Depressed, "downhearted; low spirits."
C. Stress, "effect of exerting force or pressure."
D. All of the above.
E. None of the above

Every day you take a quiz. Some days you will
have a pop quiz every hour! You will have days
ranging from A-E and back again. Hopefully you
will have more "E" days than not. Hopefully, you
will remember your loved one takes the same
daily quiz.

Here's to an "E Day" for everybody!

"This experience has put an entirely new perspective on life—talk about your paradigm shift!"

The baby monitor was placed on the dresser in Mother's bedroom and the receiver was placed on the nightstand in mine. When I heard her softly snuffling and snoring, I knew I was hearing a good night's sleep. Once I heard her mumbling in a sing song rhythm, almost as if she was reciting a poem. The next morning I asked her if she remembered her night. She told me she was naming the relatives on her family tree. She was remembering her history to stay connected to the present. So we took time for family stories and I was once more the little girl on her lap mesmerized by my eccentric great aunts and uncles.

Time has an amazing way of expanding and contracting. Be sure to go along for the ride.

"…am happy to be putting my brain back into some gear—at least it will be out of neutral."

You will find when your brain stays in neutral, it is assimilating new thoughts, patterns, or behaviors which you need to understand. To reach these understandings, you may also find that reverse is what you need. When you are traveling a new and different road, it can be really easy to get lost. As long as you are OK with turning around and taking detours, you will always arrive.

Arriving will always happen. It's just that the destination may have changed.

"Oh my goddess, a change in my only one of few established habits?! I feel a big overhaul coming on—it's about time."

Oh how I craved big, dramatic changes. A part of me just loves learning the newness of things, people, places, ideas. How confined I felt. Being a caregiver taught me how to find pleasure in the small changes—that finesse can be as much fun as bold. And I have truly learned that drama can happen with a light touch.

There are times to be bold. There are times to be quiet. It's all a part of change.

"I am thinking I should take out insurance to cover my credit cards in case I die before Mom dies—I am thinking how I will rearrange the furniture when Mom dies—it is almost spring and I am thinking of death."

When did talking about death become a taboo? How did it happen that ignoring our ultimate ending became the accepted way? If we, as caregivers, truly want our loved ones to be as comfortable as possible, we need to break the taboo and stop ignoring death. They may want to talk about their thoughts, questions, and expectations of what is to come and you need to be easy enough with death so you can listen.

For one to be at ease, all must be at ease.

"It feels like work to try and have any fun—but am trying the pretend method and maybe it will work. I am drowning and won't even look for the life boat. Gotta go get Ma's drugs before I force myself to have some fun. I feel stuck—with Mom, with friends, with old folks, with myself."

There are days where the only color you can see is gray and even rose colored glasses won't brighten the skies. On those days, be sure to keep those rose colored glasses sitting on your nose to lift the gloom when the light peeks out. As it gets brighter, you can slip them off letting you enjoy **all** the wonderful colors.

Attitude is a frame of mind, and you have control over what's in the frame.

"Let me do the Buddhist thing and just go through it—where is the line drawn between living in the moment and obsessive behavior if the moment is always the same?"

When Dad was awake at 3 a.m., cleaning the kitchen sink for hours at a time, his compulsion became his meditation. He was so involved in the motion of his arms and hands, the swirl of the cleanser, and the rhythm, he felt a control in this action. Tension dissolved and he was happy. At first this freaked me out; however, as I saw what a profound effect this "cleaning" had on Dad, I saw it for what it was—his peace with the world.

Labels are so limiting.

"I miss being outside so much and the days are so long—I have no time to do anything because I am so tired."

Complete and utter fatigue. Numbing tiredness. It will happen. Then a friend calls and offers to stay with your loved one. Or a sibling comes to visit for a week and you can move out to a motel and sleep and sleep and sleep. Just knowing there are people who love you can get you through the fatigue. You will still be tired, but knowing you are loved can get you to the other side of any problem.

Knowing yourself can be the most important knowing of all.

"The first siren of the day—I suppose we will hear many of them today. With a big holiday AND a full moon tomorrow—I think they are in for a very busy time."

What do you do with holidays? How do you handle those "firsts" after your loved one has died? Do you keep family traditions or do you start all new traditions? Whatever feels right. There are no wrong answers here. If your answer makes your heart hurt less, than it was the right choice. The first Thanksgiving after Dad died, Mom and I decided to have a meatloaf. It was Mom's favorite. I sculpted a little turkey with the hamburger. It was a wonderful moment, seeing Mom laugh as we sat down to our hamburgturkey.

The best answer doesn't have to be a universal answer.

"Everything has taken on a gloom and doom aura and I have fallen into it. How mature, responsible and boring."

Time for a switch in perspective—stand on your head if you must, but define your problems differently. As soon as I realized gloom, doom and boring didn't equal mature and responsible, life became so much smoother. Of course, it was a lesson to be learned over and over. It's funny how switching perspectives is like that.

Gloom and Doom—good names for pet turtles, but not for describing yourself.

"The change I see in Mom from yesterday to today is nothing short of miraculous. It is a most amazing transformation from yesterday when she was sleeping, sleeping, sleeping, not getting out of her chair, completely out of it."

Searching for patterns in your loved one's behavior keeps you detached. Recognizing patterns keeps you involved and helps with the daily tasks of making life the best it can be. One road makes "searching" the goal. The other makes "living" the goal. Both roads are useful if you make sure the road you choose to walk that day, that hour, is an intentional choice.

Expectations stop you from experiencing the highs and lows of the moment.

"A scrawny little squirrel is sitting out here chomping away on mushrooms and other fungus—he seems to know I am in this cage and can't hurt him. The crows are getting louder and more are gathering. It is a crow convention!"

It can be so difficult to sit still long enough to see and hear the every day happenings—harder still to absorb and enjoy them. With your mind leaping ahead to what still needs to be done or your mind feeling cold without room to hold yet another thought, the beauty of life gets lost; however, it is just such beauty that can fortify you and when retold can fortify and calm your loved one. Take time to sit on your front porch.

Nature supplies us with hints to enrich our lives. Are we listening?

"I put my notice in today. I know Mom is happy—and I will be glad, too."

Learning to follow your gut instinct offers you a wonderful decision making tool. Not the only tool, but not one to be ignored. I knew the day was coming when my full-time occupation would be as Mom's caregiver—the day itself was chosen by a gut reaction. The month gave us time to assimilate the change and within a couple of weeks of being home, Mom was admitted into the hospital and the last year of her journey had begun.

Don't ignore that tug in your belly. It is trying to tell you something.

"So back out on the front porch after a relaxing hour in the pool—believe it or not. The water was so warm—it felt good, good, good."

Watching a spider repair her beautiful, round web, I realized that, I too, was in the midst of repairing my "web" after the storm. There was so much to learn, so many lessons to remember and to honor. The persistence and creativity of the spider were two of many lessons which aided me, the caregiver, to make it through that time of grief and begin to heal.

Only when we acknowledge insights do they truly become ours.

"Ma is going to bed—the TV is off—what bliss! I need the quiet."

Caregiving presents us with opportunities to really, really appreciate the gifts which come to us every day. It also changes the size of things! What may have been a small gift has now become a huge, gigantic, humongous present. An undisturbed hour to read. A nap that ends naturally, not because of a crisis. A phone conversation which has time for pauses between the thoughts. A good laugh with a good friend. Or, maybe, caregiving doesn't change the size of things at all. It—caring and giving—just allows us to see what is genuine.

Do you know what you really need and what you really want? Do you know that sometimes they are the same?

"The last day of June and a thunderstorm has just rolled through. It is still raining and the grass looks so green. It is hard to believe it is real."

As dangerous as thunderstorms are, with their lightening and wind, they are also that beautiful with their black swirling clouds and natural fireworks. After they have rolled through, it feels so clean and so fresh. So, too, is the relationship between a loved one and the caregiver— dangerous and beautiful with the time after that feels so fresh. Without the heaviness or tension felt before the storm or the storm's cycle, we would never be refreshed. That can be hard to believe, too.

There must be contrast, or we could not see.

"I feel more grounded now, but not stuck—being here for Ma has done that for me."

There is an unbelievable time, during the fear and the pain, when your actions as a caregiver just click and, thankfully, you feel the role fit. This comfortable fit then enables you to say "Yes," to the intense question, "Can I do this?" There will surely be days when the fit is a bit snug through the shoulders; however, you now know the comfortable fit is always there waiting for you.

For a role to fit, you must define the role, not let it define you.

"How I love cycles! If I picture patterns in a circle or a spiral they are beautiful, comforting visions—however, if I envision the patterns in a linear manner they feel so boring and plodding."

How do you picture your life as a caregiver? Knowing your approach to this role allows you to discern the differences between necessary and unnecessary suffering by your loved one, and by yourself. Remembering cycles occur not only physically, but spiritually and mentally, provides us with more opportunities to help. More ways to alleviate fear. More ways to offer peace.

Even beautiful spirals can make you dizzy.

"Mom has come out onto the porch—so the energy has truly changed—her busy mind can really do that."

We would discuss the pony looking into the neighbor's window. Mom knew it wasn't real, but didn't believe it wasn't there—after all, she could **see** that white pony trotting around the yard with her own eyes. She would describe everything in wonderful detail, than look at me out of the corner of her eye to see what I would do, how I would react. I would ask her to tell me what her pony was doing now, because I couldn't see him and I needed her help. She would laugh and continue her narrative. We sat on our front porch and she escorted me into her world.

Pulling together what you see, what you know, and what you believe, brings balance to your life.

"Mom is sleeping almost all the time now. She has called me Duanne/Dad quite a few times lately, but then changes it immediately."

Changes—there will be many of them during your time as caregiver. Some to your loved one, others to yourself. Some changes strip away the layers of protection and indifference which are covering your lives. These changes bring a sharp focus to every day experiences. Some changes leave you wondering, reassessing and questioning the foundation of your life. And then some changes expose layers of yourself which may surprise you. Your job, right now, is to juggle these changes. You will drop some of them, but you know, with practice it gets better.

Without changes, our passage through life would be impossible.

"She takes over my friends and asks me questions all the time. She is trying to live my life as hers. It makes it a bit too crowded."

Of course she wanted to share my life. It helped her to be involved with the world. It helped her to be interested in the antics of friends and family. It pushed me to understand when she needed me to talk or when she needed me to just be there with a kiss for the top of her head.

Feeling crowded means your back is up against the wall. So give yourself some space, take the wall down, don't build it higher.

"So my impatience with Mom is all fear based. Well, sure it is, but of what? That it will be my fault when she dies? The whole taking care of her—can I do it?"

On my dark days, my tired days, I gave myself credit for too much power, too much control, then doubted I could live up to these incredible expectations. I had to constantly remind myself I could do "it"—as long as I knew in my heart that "it" was honoring Mother during this journey and **not** healing her. I could not stop my mother from taking this journey. Protecting Mom just enough to allow her to continue enjoying life—that had to be the goal.

Impatience—whether with yourself or another— saps your energy.

"Mom came out of her room last night wondering where the baby who was sitting on the floor in her bedroom came from. Although she knew there wasn't a baby, she is still not really convinced it wasn't there."

How frightening it must be to doubt your own senses! When your loved one sees a baby sitting there on the floor in front of them, when they hear that baby cry, how can it not be there? Yet their rational mind tells them there is no baby. How they fight to find what is real—they fight with themselves and then they may fight with you. Imagine not being able to trust yourself.

If you can't trust yourself, how can you trust others?

"Time goes so fast I can't keep up with it! Mom has been admitted to the hospital and is now back home. I didn't quit my job any too soon, that's for sure."

Decision maker. I found this to be one of the biggest hats I wore as a caregiver. Sometimes it was so huge, it fell down and covered my eyes. Panic ensued. How could I make decisions without being able to see? It wasn't easy, but I realized when I looked within myself, the best answers were there waiting for me. I read books. I asked questions. I talked to family and friends. Then I sat quietly with the information gathered to make my best decisions.

Don't waste time or energy by second guessing yourself.

"It is 3:15 am. Just got Mom to the bathroom and I can't get back to sleep."

What we take for granted can turn into the most complicated challenges. When it came to bathroom use, there was a progression from Depends, to ringing a bell in the middle of the night, to baby monitor for those times she didn't want to call for me, to the bedside commode. Introduce the commode as soon as you can—it can prolong independence for your loved one. Just two things, always monitor what's happening and buy a gazillion disposable gloves!

Proactive thinking will minimize reactive doing.

*"Stuck deep, deep, deep in the land of waiting—
for not feeling so responsible for everything."*

Admitting I wasn't responsible for everything—and
believing it—equaled being unstuck, no matter
how many "deeps" were written. For me, writing
a journal developed the muscle needed to flip
feelings from ones which pulled me down to ones
which raised me up. However you do it, find a
way to examine your feelings. We can change our
attitudes.

*Today I will wait, consciously aware of all my
feelings. Tomorrow I will wait while listening to
stories and sharing laughter.*

"Maybe as I get less scared of taking care of Mom, the better I will be at handling it. Of course, it's easier when she appears better."

It was summer. It was Florida. Mom was cold. We were both asking, "Why?" We were both hoping the answer would give us the fix. We did the obvious—turned the air conditioner off, wrapped her in an afghan, and put her in sweats. Mom was still cold. Then I found a stocking hat with matching scarf and fingerless gloves in a bargain bin at the store. The ensemble had bright stripes of wild, neon colors and Mom loved them. She wore them constantly. She was not only physically warmed, but wrapped in my warm love. We grinned, as did the nurses.

When you cannot cure the disease, you alleviate the symptoms.

"Mom had an exciting night last night, getting up to let dead dogs out and listening to a party of all dead family members. She has so much going on."

I can't imagine how terrifying it must be to know you can't trust your own eyes or ears. Knowing your beloved pet is barking and wagging his tail to say he needs to go out, but also knowing he has been gone for 35 years has got to make you wonder what is happening. Not being able to ignore his needs, you get out of bed and go to the door to let him out. As the caregiver, I had to step back to remember the whole picture and the goal of keeping Mom safe. I would lock the deadbolt, but not the door itself, so when she flipped the locks, one was always being locked as the other was being unlocked. It kept her inside. It kept her safe. It gave me some peace of mind.

Seeing is not always believing.

"Being here for Mom is 'doing'. Guess I am just having trouble balancing my health and well-being and hers."

Balance. One of the most important words in caregiving. The caregiver must balance their needs with their loved ones needs. And as the journey progresses, this balance is more difficult to achieve. There is a harmony which can be maintained, even when the balance is tenuous, for this journey is a natural one and our love is the perfect balance.

The most difficult times need the strength of your deepest held beliefs

"We were discussing the meaning of love and the place of compromise in that love. Mom said one needed to compromise, because if you love somebody, you would rather be a little miserable with them then not be miserable and be by yourself. "

This conversation was so important to both of us—her outlook on life and love and my ability to finally understand. It gave me the most essential insight for the management of her care. She did not want to be alone, and this, I could give.

Listening with your whole self, while turning off the rest of the world, can be the greatest gift—for both of you.

"I am trying to keep Mom informed and sharing with her, and still keeping boundaries. She can't tell the difference between us. How do I keep her involved, but out?"

I was frantic about "keeping boundaries," about not losing myself on the path we were walking. Then I called it desperation, but now I know it was denial. Denial of losing my Mom. Denial of losing control—hard to lose what was never mine. If only I could control our boundaries, I could control what happened to us within those boundaries. Luckily, I had the time and opportunity to move through the denial process, learning as I went.

Sometime the right answer is, "I can't."

"It is one of those wonderful days where the pieces are all fitting and even if the picture is not what I thought it would be, it is a fine picture—and I am content. I will take this break quite thankfully! There is so much to learn and contemplate."

When the picture turns into a scene you hadn't anticipated, you can curse the new terrain and not budge, or you can step into the scene with both feet and take the new path. Being ready for changes and following where they may lead can make this trip of living and dying less overwhelming and more comforting.

Just because the scenery has changed, doesn't mean it is the wrong picture.

"Ma opened her therapy gloves from Sally the very first thing on Christmas morning and then wore them the rest of the day! What a great idea."

Looking back at the last time a special event happened can be both wonderful and painful. The pain that comes from what you did or did not say, from what you did or did not do, can be the worst pain. Learning from these memories, you can now leave the people in your life with a smile and "I love you," even if you are just leaving to buy some milk.

Sometimes the smallest gesture can make the biggest difference

"The weather is perfect. Mom is talking nonstop. I stubbed my toe. It is nice to know some things don't change."

In all the turmoil, during all the changes, there will be those little moments which will become endearing memories. Some of them will not be so endearing while they are happening, but later, when thinking back to the journey taken; those moments will be cherished—even nonstop talking.

We honor life by the memories we keep.

"Mom has been getting up more and NOT using the lift on her chair, which is a step up. And she is just loving those ear phones. I think those have to be the best present I have ever given her—and to think, it is good for both of us."

There are so many ways to enhance life. Some are esoteric and some are just down to earth common sense. Mixing these two techniques gives a special joy to every day. Wireless earphones for the TV. A big hug. A tartan plaid bib for mealtime. A shared memory. Tubes of bright lipstick. And, of course, chocolate chip cookie dough!

Can't you just hear the smiles in our voices when we are being playful?

"Got Ma a new shower chair today, so now need to put it together. I am sure the higher legs will make it easier for her to get in the shower and up and down. Today is one of those days where it is just a fog for her. Tomorrow should be lots better, if the pattern continues."

Sometimes, the smallest fix in the physical world can make a huge difference to our outlook in the emotional one. Remembering how interconnected our worlds are—mental, emotional, physical and spiritual—is so important in caregiving. When we make a change to one, it will resonate within the others. Being more self-reliant can feel just as good as a nice hot shower—maybe even better.

Stopping allows the fog to slip away and sometimes this works better than trying to fight your way through it.

"Didn't go to the movies. By the time I got Ma's new shower chair put together and she practiced using it and getting to 'trust' it, I decided to stay home and read."

Patience. Patience. Patience. The more we fight problems, the more exhausted we become. And that includes everybody—the caregiver, the loved one, and the occasional observer. It was a great idea to practice using the shower chair. Not such a great idea thinking there was only one way to approach the problem. Let your loved one work out Plan A. If it works, fantastic. If it doesn't, Plan B will be so much more acceptable.

Even going with the flow can be tiring, so don't do the breaststroke.

"I am being overpowered by Mom's reality—fear and loathing and quiet suffering."

Just acknowledging that it is a very dark day can help lift the darkness, at least around the edges. Some days the only thing to be done is to take these dark hours and live them the best you can. Being there for each other helps keep the fear from completely taking over.

Taking no action can be a significant act.

"Mom is in her TV room counting and recounting her pills and jabbering a mile a minute."

Doing an every day task can restore a sense of normalcy to daily life. Even if the task isn't quite completed, or is completed 2 or 3 times, the doing can have a calming effect—not only for the loved one, but the caregiver, too. And jabbering can be a fine way to restore normalcy.

What is "normal," if not something that helps us feel safe?

"Mom liked her Valentine's Day surprise. I need to tell her I love her more—not just echo it back to her."

I had to learn how important it was for me to tell Mother, "I love you." She was happy when I showed her my love by actions, but she really needed to hear it—especially when I would leave the house. She didn't want the last words she heard from me to be anything other than, "I love you," and neither did I.

If we are lucky, important lessons last a lifetime.

"Almost had a panic attack when I was sitting here without any real thing in mind to do. I don't know how to stop and relax—the stopping part, not so bad. The relaxing part, pretty awful."

It took me many months to remember how to relax. After Mom died, I would be out with friends and then jump up with car keys in hand ready to leave. The buzzer in my head would go off telling me time was up and I needed to get home immediately. Then I would remember there was no rush and collapse back into my chair. It was a painful process, but a much needed one.

It takes time to redefine your role in life.

"I need to grasp the large picture—what I am 'being', not what I am 'doing'. I am 'being' a daughter, not I am 'waiting for the next crisis'. What a different slant it puts on it all. I am being myself, and part of being me includes waiting."

Waiting can be so difficult, especially when you don't know for what you are waiting. But keeping it in perspective and not allowing the waiting to overshadow the rest of life can bring waiting into balance. The times we are waiting are the commas in the sentences of life.

There is a good reason why we are called human beings and not human doings.

"Poor Mom! She is asleep. Two days ago she asked me if 'Lawrence' was my brother's name. Man, that got my heart big time. She knew right away it was. Just a glimmer of not knowing. As she says, and it is true—we can still laugh."

Incredulous. Disbelief. Relief. Humor. In just a matter of seconds, all those emotions were expressed on my Mother's face. Her nonverbal gave me more insight into her feelings than all her words could express. Being in tune with all her emotions helped me to respond as needed—fortissimo or pianissimo.

Playing heart strings can make beautiful music. It's just that the heart isn't always so easily tuned.

"Mom is not ready for Hospice, but when it happens, we will be there."

The comfort of having a plan cannot be overrated—as long as it is not written in stone, is very, very flexible, and is one of many. Even if it doesn't sound like much of a plan, it will be a cushion to fall back on. A little something to break the fall. Just make sure you include your loved one in the decision making process as much as possible. It needs to be a cushion for two.

Knowing there is a cushion waiting for you while you are falling feels good.

"Mom really had a bad week, but seems to be on the upswing! Some of her friends didn't come over at Mom's request. When she talked to them on the phone, she told them she didn't have much longer to live. She said, 'I just wanted to warn them'."

Mom's bluntness amazed me and made so many of her friends feel uneasy. She did what felt best for her. I was so proud of her. She didn't want euphuisms, so we didn't use euphemisms. She was going to die and, together, we wrote parts of her obituary. Of course, everybody walks a different path towards death. Mom's path was straight and by walking with her, I honored her. Whether the path is straight and smooth or hilly and rocky, hiking boots are a necessity as you walk with your loved one.

There is no communicating without listening.

"A whole lifetime has passed since I wrote a single word. Mother has been under Hospice care, here at home, since April 5th."

We need to believe that exactly what we need is both out there and within ourselves. We just need to be ready to welcome what we need with open arms.

Accepting help does not mean we have failed.

"When I go with the flow and quit looking for excuses to act like a 'butthead', then things are certainly better!"

Trying to rationalize anger by getting upset with all those little, inconsequential things that go wrong, is unhealthy for everyone. So is containing the anger. That doesn't work either and that uncontrolled anger oozes out contaminating other moments of our lives. The best we can do is figure out what we are really, truly angry about, and then change our perceptions—use all that energy to find healthy alternatives, not to remain angry.

Choosing what to think is as possible as choosing what to do. Not as easy, but certainly possible.

"I am personally fighting with depression and despair. The first month taking care of Mom fulltime wasn't bad, but I am locked into the house and find myself waiting/wanting it to be over, and feeling guilty about what that means. I think, who am I to complain? She's the one dying!"

Depression and despair are debilitating. The more we ignore them, the more powerful they become. They scream, "Look at me! Look at me!" As we twist and turn not listening to the screams, we also block out the significant messages we are being given. Loving somebody and yet wanting "it to be over" are not mutually exclusive. Just very hard to reconcile.

Sometimes the hardest thing to do is just listen.

"We have just shredded 2 large garbage bags of bills and junk mail. I sorted and Ma shredded. It was a project that really made her feel involved—hope I can find more like that."

Mom destroyed all of her debts, which had been paid in full, and junk mail, which nobody wanted, and turned them into packing material, which would protect valuable items. Talk about symbols!

Making useless useful—a great skill or…magic.

"It is a beautiful day—live it to the fullest—no matter what that means today!"

And the same thing applies to the ugly days, for we really don't know which day will be the last.

If all choices are deliberate choices, the day is well spent.

"It is all wearing thin—so this is when I really need to suck it up and use some of these beliefs I hold. Dig deep into me and pull up the love and peace and mindfulness. Whoa, don't tell me it's time to practice what I preach?!?"

Humor in all its manifestations saved me many a day, especially when I was poking fun at myself. It is impossible to clench your jaw when smiling, chuckling or down right laughing.

Unclenching is a wonderful relief.

"The dynamics of this relationship between Mother and Daughter are once again changing. I do feel as if it is an adversarial relationship—all I do is deny her food and keep her quiet and feed her, etc., etc. And all this she does not want or wants to do herself. I try to keep her safe and she wants to see how far she can push it."

Two completely different objectives. Both completely legitimate. In the long run, they are reaching for the same thing—a quality of life worth living.

There really can be many right answers to the same question.

"Mother is back in bed. The woman who is tired of fighting it all has shown up today. When she doesn't have the energy to put on the happy face, then I know she really doesn't have the energy."

Being able to interpret your loved one's nonverbal communications can save the energy needed to accomplish the important things in life—holding a hand, smiling at the birds, saying I love you.

What is not done speaks as loudly as what is.

"Mom asked if I wanted my brother to call me if she died while I was gone. I told her yes, and that Judy and I would just drive down from Tenn. That brain of hers just never stops."

We talked of death and the things Mom wanted. She wanted the ashes of their beloved cat, Jay Jay, buried with her and Dad. She wanted to be remembered as a person who loved many and was loved by many. We talked of things she didn't want. She didn't want a funeral or a memorial service. She didn't want us paying "one cent more" than had already been paid to the funeral home. She needed to know these requests would be honored and I needed to honor them.

You can't anticipate all the questions, so don't expect to have all the answers.

"I got a booklet about the signs of physical decline, but nothing about the anxiety and/or talks with spirits."

There are many resources out there to help you with your role as caregiver, but that doesn't mean you won't be using the learn as-you-go-plan! One of the most important lessons I learned about my Mother was: If she could tell me what was confusing her or what hurt, it lightened her load. And one of the most important lessons I learned about myself was: There were days I could listen just fine, but there were days when listening made me a little more confused or hurt a little more. As long as I didn't deny either of these days, both were OK. When I denied how I was feeling, everything went down hill.

When you are reaching out to others, make sure you don't turn your back on yourself.

"If we make it through the hurricane season it will be a miracle—Mom is sooooo freaked and so of course, the first storm is headed straight for us. I want her to feel as safe as possible, so I'm retelling her as often as need be what we have in the Hurricane Room and that we are ready."

I emptied the walk-in closet, making it into a little sitting room to wait out the storms. It was equipped with everything—chairs, a battery driven TV, lanterns, a radio, enough batteries for the neighborhood, extra meds, all our important papers and lots of peanut butter. It helped, but Mom was still pretty scared. I bought a generator. It helped, but Mom was still scared. As much as I wanted to relieve all her fears, I couldn't, because I could not control the storms.

We cannot control the storms, we can only prepare.

"A band of rain is coming through right now; Mom is in bed; I am trying to make sure she feels as safe as possible, but she is so worried. Man, this will be a challenging few months."

The world will become so small. Our world became that nest in the walk-in closet. We would visit it daily. We would practice what to do. I would sleep on the floor in her bedroom. We would talk and talk and talk about the chances a hurricane would hit. We were fighting "F's"—her fear, my frustration—and trying to change them into "A's"—her absence of fear, my acceptance of the situation.

Learning can take place anytime, anywhere—even without grades being given.

"I love seeing her being more honest and vocal, and it does make for some surprises."

Changes in your loved one's personality are not unusual. And these changes may happen for many different reasons—medication, dementia, lack of oxygen to the brain, loss of inhibitions. Caregivers need to be ready for any changes, whether they are positive or negative. Many of Mom's changes were ones I liked to see happen. I never knew if Mom did.

Unanswered questions may always be just that— unanswered questions.

"Mom and Larry had a great time together. He even cooked a dinner for them which they ate out on the front porch and they ate by candlelight. Isn't that the coolest?"

My brother would come to stay with Mom so I could leave for some much needed R&R. They were wonderful times for all of us. My friends would make all the decisions so I could just sit back and relax. Mom was given quality time alone with her son. Larry gave us both time away from each other and was able to spend some special moments with Mom. We were all making new memories.

Being away is necessary so you can return 100%.

"Mom has a urinary tract infection. Her numbers on kidney function are really bad. Her BUN is 73.4 and the normal range is 7-18."

Some moments will be so vivid and they will be as varied as the people living them. Those "aha" moments, those pictures which will last forever, those pictures which fade with time, but have left an emotional print on your soul—they will be different for everyone and they will be life changing, life enriching.

The connections are there. We must let ourselves feel them.

"Mom is back in bed sleeping. The good news—
no morphine since 4pm yesterday and no pain
since 7pm yesterday. The bad news—she had an
incredible panic attack last night. I called Hospice.
Mom talked to the nurse and then she seemed
to be better. She needed the authority person to
let her know we were doing the right thing. She
said she was afraid she would lose her mind and
never find her way back. We talked; I read to her,
I held her hand. Those attacks are hard to watch
and worse yet, I am sure, to be the one going
through them. She didn't want to go back to bed
this morning, even though she was falling asleep
in her chair, because she thought the 'evil' would
come back. So, I smudged her room with sage
Susan had sent me and explained to her about
the Navajo use of sage and protection. I think it
has helped, as she went in there, could smell that
wonderful smell and fell asleep. And as for me,
the smell is so calming—I wonder why I haven't
done this sooner."

The right help comes at the right time.

"When Mom starts to talk about being afraid of everything coming back—pain and/or 'the crazies'—I tell her we aren't fortune tellers, so let's be happy about the good happening RIGHT NOW. We will see how long that will bring her back to here. After all, the here and now is not that great for her and she has never been one to focus on the now or the positive. I am trying to do both for both."

Who was bothered more by the "crazies"—Mother or me? It was a close call. I had expected her venturing out of the here and now to be a happy time for her. It was not. Where do you go when everywhere you go is scary? There was no answer as to where as long as we were together. Together as long as she needed me by her side.

Knowing when to back away can be the most difficult knowing and the most difficult to do.

"Susan, I have just smudged Mom's room with sage you sent me to keep away the 'evil things'— an indication of how things are going here. Learning new things, rejoicing in old things."

Remember to use all the resources available to make your loved one feel more comfortable, no matter how strange you may think those resources are. It is important to not only relieve the physical pain, but to make anxiety more bearable and to soothe as many fears as you can. These resources can be so many things—books to read aloud, music to calm breathing, together remembering good times, medications to still the pain, visitors to bring love and, new pillows to bring smiles.

There is no here and now without the past and future.

"She seems to be pretty good—talking more and thankful for the 'magic medicine'—she says it makes her brain think better. Man, I better get some of this stuff!"

Some days it felt impossible to think. Some days it didn't just feel impossible to think, it was impossible to think. The best I could do on those days was to go on cruise control, rely on habits and be as aware of my surroundings as possible. I may have felt as if I had become a robot, but if that's what it took to empty the bedside commode and fix meals, it was OK! I knew the magic would return.

My magic is humor. What is yours?

"Good news—I have hired somebody to come in 2 nights a week, so not only will I get a good night's sleep, but I can go out for a cup of coffee and take a trip around the store—hot diggity dog!"

Exhausted. Dragging one foot in front of the other. Making one more bowl of oatmeal. Tears hiding behind the eyes, just waiting to spill over. Stumbling into the bedroom with the breakfast tray I say, "Breakfast is served, Madam." Looking at each other, looking at the oatmeal, looking back at each other. Both of us breaking into laughter. No more exhaustion. Tears laughed away. Love everywhere.

Laughter the best medicine? You betcha!

"The transfusion is tomorrow—the poor little thing looks so bad. I sure hope this will make her more comfortable."

At first Mom didn't want anything to do with making the decision about getting a transfusion or not, but with her wonderful oncologist patiently explaining and coaxing her to really think about what she wanted, she did just that, and made her choice. Making this decision actually had a better effect on her well-being than the medical procedure. We relearned so much from the Doctor's approach—patience, patience, patience, and how soothing being responsible and "in control" can feel.

Decision making is healing.

"She is tough, but seems to understand and accept more now that she realizes there is no cure for the anemia. Her anxiety levels have been the worst; however, her meds have helped both of us immensely."

I was surprised at the fear my Mother expressed as her death drew closer. A struggle between her spiritual beliefs and her emotions. It was a struggle I hadn't anticipated, for her faith was strong; however, peace became difficult for her to find. It was at that moment I truly understood what an intimate and singular journey our lives are. I could hold her hand and give her all my love, but she had to walk the path by herself, as we all, ultimately, do. I wanted to protect her so much and save her from her fear. Understanding that I couldn't, is one of my life's biggest lessons.

We cannot learn another's lesson—only our own.

"I am glad to be here during this journey, and look forward to coming back to my life when this chapter closes."

Ah, yes, "coming back to my life." Too many wonderful and profound events had taken place to "go back." And what had I been doing if not living my life? How did I lose sight of such important lessons? My life hadn't been put on hold, even if it felt as if it had. How my life was lived every day is what mattered.

How chapters are interconnected is what makes a terrific book, or not. Same goes for our lives.

"My world has become so minute, it is enormous!"

As the physical world shrinks to become only the bedroom and the kitchen, the inner world expands to many place—places to rest, places to laugh, places to share, places to be alone. Be sure to go to all the places you can. Take your loved one with you, if they want to go. This is a time when the traveling is imperative, because staying home is so important.

Life is a paradox.

"Can not get away, or don't want to be far away now. Death is such a different journey for everybody, but I still know that here is where I am supposed to be and am so glad that I can be here and that I am! It is funny what little thoughts will cause the most guilt or the most sorrow or the best memory. Every day is a learning experience—can't ask for more than that."

It is true that losing a loved one brings sorrow and guilt. It is also true that recognizing these feelings must happen—sooner or later. You can not say you are sorry or share a favorite memory, unless you acknowledge your feelings and thoughts. And your pain resulting from the guilt and the sorrow will not heal if you don't first acknowledge you have these feelings.

Being aware of your emotions is the only way to feel them.

"Mother is now on oxygen full-time, just had a transfusion, and is on anti-anxiety meds. She is taking her time on her journey and, luckily, it has been relatively pain free. I continue to learn more every day—it reaffirms how amazing life truly is."

To help a loved one meet the end of their life is a difficult, frustrating, unbelievable, amazing honor. There will be pain and joy, uncertainty and peace. When all is offered with a giving heart, the journey is bathed in love—for both you and your loved one.

Accepting death allows you to embrace life.

"So now the circle has been completed. Mother died Aug 1 at 4:30 am. It seems all too real and not at all real. So natural—just the way it goes for all of us."

I miss my Mama. I miss her wit. I miss her intelligence. I miss our talks of, "What if...?" I miss when our eyes locked and we both, stubbornly, swore we were right. She was my mother and I loved her so very much.

Never forget to show your love, no matter how you choose to do it.

LaVergne, TN USA
14 March 2011
219912LV00001B/3/P